THE AZTECS

DONNA WALSH SHEPHERD
THE AZTECS

Franklin Watts   New York   London   Toronto   Sydney   A First Book

Cover photograph copyright © Robert Frerck/Odyssey/Chicago
Photographs copyright © : The Bodleian Library, Oxford (from Ms. Arch. Seld. A.1): pp. 13 (fol 2R), 34 (fol 61R), 37 (fol 37R); New York Public Library, Picture Collection: pp. 10, 50; North Wind Picture Archives: pp. 15, 21, 28, 38 top, 52; Robert Frerck/Odyssey/Chicago: pp. 3, 19, 29, 36, 56, 57; University of Utah Press, Salt Lake City, Ut.: pp. 24, 32 bottom, 39, 42, 44, 47; American Museum of Natural History: pp. 32 top (#1735-2), 38 bottom (#1802-2); Lauros-Giraudon/ Art Resource, N.Y.: p. 40.

Library of Congress Cataloging-in-Publication Data

Shepherd, Donna Walsh.
The Aztecs / by Donna Walsh Shepherd.
p.   cm.—(A First book)
Includes bibliographical references and index.
Summary: Describes the Aztec civilization, its customs, and religion.
ISBN 0-531-20064-7
1. Aztecs—Juvenile literature. [1. Aztecs.   2. Indians of Mexico.]   I. Title.   II. Series.
F1219.S5   1992
972'.018—dc20   91-28397
                                                       CIP   AC

First Paperback Edition 1992
0-531-15634-6

This is dedicated to my dear sons
Chadney, Shane, and Aaron

with whom I have climbed the Pyramid of the Sun and the
Pyramid of the Moon, walked down the Avenue of the Dead
to the Temple of Quetzalcoatl, and listened for the old Aztec
chants that hang just behind the sun

CONTENTS

THE AZTECS

THE AZTECS TRAVELED FROM THEIR LEGENDARY
ISLAND AZTLAN TO A MOUNTAIN VALLEY IN THEIR SEARCH
FOR A NEW HOME. FOUR PRIESTS LED THE WAY TO
THE LAND PROMISED BY THE GOD HUITZILOPOCHTLI,
WHOSE IMAGE IS BORNE BY THE FIRST PRIEST. THE
GOD TOLD THEM THEY WOULD FOUND A CITY AND
GROW INTO A POWERFUL CIVILIZATION.

FINDING A HOME

In 1168 the North American continent was very sparsely inhabited. Forest and prairie stretched from coast to coast. There were no towns, no cities. Columbus would not arrive for more than three hundred years.

Legend tells us it was at that time, somewhere in northern Mexico in a sacred cave, the Aztec priests found that a new god had been born. That god was Huitzilopochtli (Weet-zeel-o-potch-tly), or Hummingbird Wizard. He became the god of sun and war. Huitzilopochtli told the people they needed to leave their home in Aztlan, Place of the Herons, and search for a new place to live. In their new home they would build a great and powerful civilization. He then gave them a new name for their new life: the Aztec Indians also became known as the Mexicas.

The Aztecs were a very religious people. They strongly believed it was very important to do as their gods ordered. They abandoned their home in the north and began walking to the south, searching for a new home. They built a special container for Huitzilopochtli, and four *teomamaque,* or god carriers, carried Hummingbird Wizard with them on their long and wandering journey.

Along the way, Hummingbird Wizard told them stories of what their new life would be like. He told them about the new city they would build. It would be on an island in the center of a lake. Willows, cypresses, reeds, and grasses would grow there. Fish and ducks would live in the lake. It would be a place of beauty and plenty. They would know they had found the right place for their new home when they saw a prickly pear cactus with red fruit, growing out of a rock. Perched on top of the cactus would be an eagle eating a serpent.

For more than 150 years, the Aztecs wandered, looking for their new home. Sometimes they stopped for a year or two and planted corn and other crops, but they always moved on, looking for the sign Hummingbird Wizard had promised them. Finally, they came into the central valley of Mexico, which had previously been controlled by the mighty Toltec Indians. But that civilization had broken apart and scattered. Now many new

THE AZTECS, ALSO KNOWN AS MEXICAS, WERE
TOLD TO LOOK FOR AN EAGLE PERCHED ON
A CACTUS AS A SIGN THAT THEY HAD REACHED
THE PLACE WHERE THEY WERE TO SETTLE.
EARLY MEXICA LEADERS ARE SHOWN
SEATED, SURROUNDING THE EAGLE.

tribes were coming into the area. Because the Aztecs were the last to arrive, they got the worst land.

At first the Aztecs settled on Chapultepec, or Grasshopper Hill. But their new neighbors didn't want them there. The other tribes considered the Aztecs *barbarians,* uncivilized, rough people. One day the Culhua tribe tricked the Aztec warriors into leaving their hill and then captured the women and children. To get their families back, the Aztecs agreed to move to Tizapan, which was infested with poisonous snakes. The Culhuas hoped the snakes would kill the Aztecs, but instead the Aztecs killed and ate the snakes.

Their enemies grew to know and respect the Aztecs for their capabilities in battle. When the Culhua Indians needed help to defeat the Xochimilco tribe, they turned to the Aztecs. After the victorious battle, Hummingbird Wizard told the Aztec priests to ask the Culhua chief for one of his daughters, saying they would treat her like a goddess. Because the Culhuas thought she would marry the leader of the Aztecs, they agreed. When the young woman came to live with the Aztec tribe, they gave her their highest honor: they sacrificed her to the gods and skinned her. They believed this would help her become a goddess.

Soon the Culhuas came to visit the chief's daughter, and the Aztecs planned a special ceremony. Inside the dark, smoky temple, the Culhua chief suddenly re-

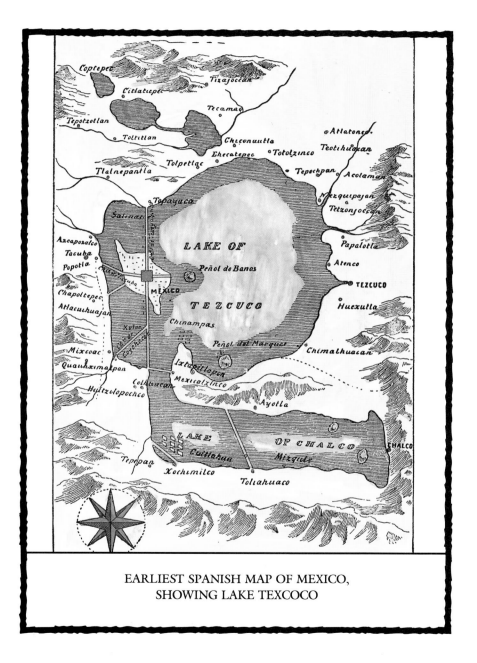

EARLIEST SPANISH MAP OF MEXICO,
SHOWING LAKE TEXCOCO

alized that the figure dancing before him was an Aztec priest wearing his daughter's skin. In anger at what had happened to the young woman, the Culhuas attacked the Aztecs. The Aztecs fled and hid on a useless, swampy island in the middle of Lake Texcoco, Lake of the Moon.

On the island, confused and homeless once again, the Aztecs had nothing. They went to the water's edge to catch frogs and snakes for food. There they saw a prickly pear cactus with red fruit, growing out of a rock. On top of the cactus sat an eagle eating a serpent. After more than 150 years of wandering, the Aztecs were finally home.

THE NEW CITY

When the Aztecs realized that they had found their new home, the first thing they did was build a small temple of mud and grasses next to the cactus to honor and thank Huitzilopochtli. They named their new city Tenochtitlan (Te-notch-ti-tlan), Place of the Prickly Pear Cactus. Then they began to plan their new home so that it would became the great city Hummingbird Wizard had described to them. That was not going to be easy. How do you turn a small swampy island into a beautiful large city?

At first the Aztecs were busy just gathering food and building small mud and grass huts to live in. But they knew they needed more land, for homes, for growing food, and for a great city center.

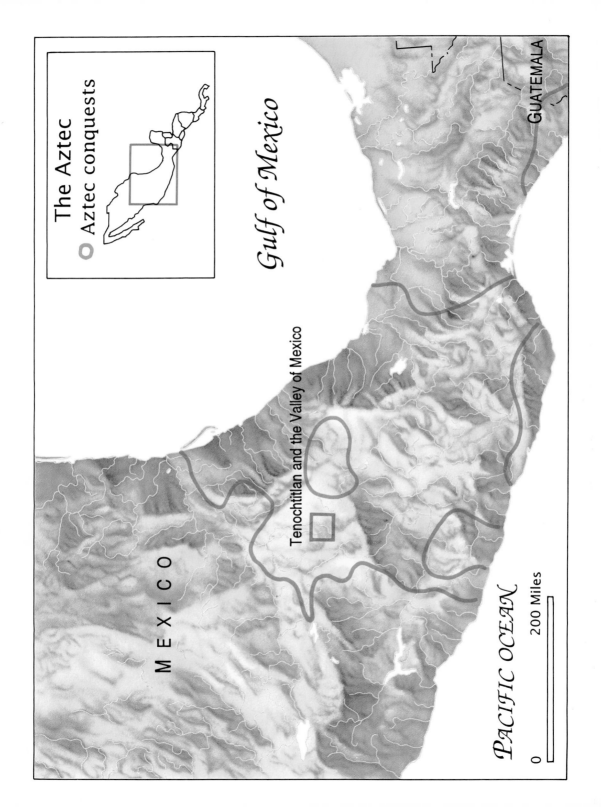

The Aztec

○ Aztec conquests

Gulf of Mexico

GUATEMALA

Tenochtitlan and the Valley of Mexico

MEXICO

PACIFIC OCEAN

0   200 Miles

AFTER REACHING THEIR NEW HOME, THE AZTECS
BEGAN BUILDING THE CITY OF TENOCHTITLAN.

The Aztecs were very clever. They built large rafts by lashing bundles of reeds together. Then they took buckets and dredged up mud and muck from the lake bottom and piled it on the rafts. This was very fertile mud and wonderful for growing vegetables. The Aztecs tied these floating gardens, called *chinampas,* to the shore, and soon the roots from the plants and trees grew to the lake floor and anchored the rafts there. They became part of the island.

Gradually, the Aztecs increased the size of their island and eventually connected it to other nearby islands. But they left pathways of water between some of the chinampas. These canals served as waterways for canoe travel and transportation. Hard-packed roadways paralleled the canals for foot travel.

The Aztecs began trading some of their fish, frogs, and vegetables to the tribes that lived on the lake shores for log and stone building material. They rebuilt Hummingbird Wizard's temple, made better houses, and began construction on the ceremonial center of town.

It was in the early fifteenth century that Aztec civilization really began to flourish and expand. The first King Moctezuma formed alliances and made trade agreements with other tribes. If a tribe would not agree to what Moctezuma wanted, the Aztecs attacked. The fierce Aztec warriors were nearly always victorious in conquering and controlling other tribes.

The Aztecs forced the other tribes to pay taxes to them. If they had no money or goods to give to the Aztecs, the other tribes had to work off their tax debt. In that way, the Aztecs got free labor to build their temples and schools, their roads and bridges.

In only a few decades, Tenochtitlan became the beautiful capital city of a large empire, as Hummingbird Wizard had prophesied. The buildings were painted a gleaming white or were polished until the stone walls

A STREET IN TENOCHTITLAN, THE
ANCIENT CITY OF MEXICO

shone like silver. Trees and flowers were everywhere, even growing from rooftops. Pools of water and canals laced through the city, and in the center was a sacred ceremonial square, dominated by the Great Pyramid.

The great pyramids of Mexico were not tombs to bury kings in, like the pyramids of Egypt; rather they were platforms for altars and temples to the gods. On top of the Great Pyramid of Tenochtitlan were two temples. On the south side, painted red and white, was the temple of Hummingbird Wizard, god of sun and war. On the north side stood the blue and white temple of Tlaloc, god of water and rain. Seven times the Aztecs enlarged and remodeled the pyramid, each time building right over the top of the old one and making it more magnificent.

Also in the center square were temples to other gods, including Quetzalcoatl (Kayt-zal-co-alt), the god of wind and learning. Quetzalcoatl's temple was round so that it would not disturb the current of the breeze. A sacrificial altar, the ball court, a school for priests and leaders, a rack for sacrificed skulls, and special places for prayer and meditation formed the sacred area, which was surrounded by a serpent wall.

Nearby was the grand palace of the king, with its zoos and gardens. Another palace, for important visitors, as well as courts of law, schools, and the houses of wealthy people were also in the center square. Some of the buildings were two stories high. But only in the center of Tenochtitlan, on the original island, was the ground strong enough to support the weight of the heavier buildings.

Off the main square was the great market. At one end of the market stood the calendar stone to mark time in the universe, and at the other end was the Tizoc stone, where soldiers gathered before battle. The market was a wonderful and exciting place. Sixty thousand people a day came to shop for food and goods from all over Mexico and Central America. The market was full of marvelous sights, colors, and smells. Each product had its own section of the market—fruits and vegetables, flowers, jewelry, precious stones, gold, birds and feathers, clothing and textiles, incense, and medicines.

Around the ceremonial center the city was divided into four districts, each with its own community government, shops, parks, schools, and temples for the lesser gods. Most people lived in one-story white stone or adobe houses with private patios and gardens, but on the outskirts of town poor people still lived in mud and grass huts.

The Aztecs were great engineers. To make travel to the mainland easier, they built three great *causeways*, with movable bridges for protection and flood control. Because the rains and melting snows washed salts from the earth into Lake Texcoco, the Aztecs built a double cov-

GOODS DISPLAYED IN THE MARKETPLACE. THE
MARKET WAS A BUSTLING, COLORFUL PLACE.

ered *aqueduct* to bring fresh spring water from Chapultepec Hill 3 miles (4.8 km) away.

The Aztecs were able to build such a beautiful, rich city from nothing because they strongly believed the gods had predicted it. They saw it as their duty to fulfill the gods' *prophecies,* and their powerful army enabled them to control other tribes and to get the goods, money, and slave power they needed.

RELIGION AND THE GODS

The Aztecs believed that their world was a gift from the gods, and that they were specially chosen to take care of that world. If they failed, the sun would stop moving across the sky, and the world would wither and die in the darkness.

They also believed that this was not the first world. Four earlier worlds had existed, and four times they were destroyed. The existence of each world was called a Sun. Legend says the First Sun was destroyed when jaguars came and ate the people of the earth. The jaguar was a symbol for the night, its spotted coat representing the night sky spotted with stars. Perhaps this was a way of saying the people perished when a comet hit the earth.

The Second Sun ended when hurricanes destroyed

the world and people were changed into monkeys. Volcanoes destroyed the Third Sun in a rain of fire. The Fourth Sun ended when a great flood swept over the earth and the people were changed to fish. Only one man and one woman survived, but they disobeyed the gods and were turned into dogs.

To get new people for the next Sun, the Sun of Movement, the god Quetzalcoatl went into the underworld and stole bones from the dead ancestors. Quetzalcoatl poured his own blood over the bones to bring them to life.

The Aztecs believed that in the beginning of time there was a mother god and a father god. These two gods had many children, who became the gods of Aztec time. Each new god ruled and controlled different things.

Quetzalcoatl was a special god, the Plumed Serpent, god of the wind. He was also the god of culture and learning, of goodness and kindness. The Aztecs believed that long ago, at the beginning of this Sun, Quetzalcoatl was betrayed by his brother and sister gods and forced to leave Mexico in disgrace. But as Quetzalcoatl sailed off to the east, he promised to return one day and lead his people.

During their search for the eagle on the cactus, the Aztecs came to a place where they believed their Sun began. From far away they saw a giant pyramid rising to the heavens. As they came to the pyramid, they were

QUETZALCOATL,
THE AZTEC
GOD OF WIND
AND LEARNING

in awe. It was in an abandoned city of many pyramids and temples. Nothing but sunlight filled the streets. Only a breeze beckoned them to prayer.

The Aztecs sensed holiness in this city and thought it surely must have been made by the gods. What men could build such beautifully colored and carved monuments, high as mountains?

They named the buildings—Pyramid of the Sun, Pyramid of the Moon, Temple of Quetzalcoatl. They named the wide street that ran the mile length of the city Avenue of the Dead, after the holy people they were sure were buried in the smaller temples on each side.

IN TEOTIHUACAN, THE PYRAMID OF THE SUN AND
AVENUE OF THE DEAD. WHEN THE AZTECS CAME ACROSS
THIS CITY, THEY WERE IN AWE OF THIS WONDROUS
PLACE OF PYRAMIDS AND TEMPLES. THEY
REGARDED IT AS A HOLY CITY, BUILT BY THE GODS.

They named the entire area Teotihuacan (Tay-o-tee-wah-can), Place of the Gods. Even after their own city of Tenochtitlan was built, the Aztec priests sometimes returned to Teotihuacan for special ceremonies.

Today we know that Teotihuacan was nearly a thousand years old in the time of the Aztecs and was not built by gods but by a culture lost to us now. In its time it was the center of a great city of a quarter of a million people.

It was there in Teotihuacan, the Aztecs believed, that one of the gods sacrificed himself for the people on a sacred fire so that the sun would move across the sky.

This began the Aztec ritual of human *sacrifice*. The sun must be fed blood for strength to fight the dark forces of the night and continue to move across the sky. And it was the Aztecs' job to save the world by providing that blood.

In the Aztec world it was an honor to give your life to the gods. Frequently, a victim was dressed to look like a particular god. When the person died, it was not a human dying but the god, once again sacrificing himself for the people. Often before sacrificing ceremonies, the victims were fed drugs so that they would not feel pain.

Most victims for sacrifice were prisoners of war. Sometimes the Aztecs fought "Flower Wars" until they had just enough victims for their sacrifices. The Aztecs believed it was only through these sacrificial deaths that life in this Sun was able to continue.

BEING BORN AZTEC

One of the happiest times in Aztec society was when a new baby was born. There was always a special naming ceremony with feasting and speeches. Fortune-tellers made predictions for the baby's future, and the baby was given miniature tools to represent his or her adult life. If a boy's father was a nobleman, the boy would be given a little shield and spear. If his father was a farmer, he would receive a special little digging stick. All girls were given small brooms and spindles.

Aztec children were raised very strictly. At home they had many chores and were taught skills such as weaving, featherworking, running a house, fishing, or farming. Children were also taught to be obedient, well-mannered, self-disciplined, and, above all, honorable.

TOP: A WOMAN CONSULTS A READER OF SIGNS.
THE ADVICE OF FORTUNE-TELLERS WAS SOUGHT
WHEN BABIES WERE BORN. BOTTOM: YOUNG
AZTEC WOMEN STUDIED WEAVING.

When children reached their early teens, they went to a formal school. Very talented commoners and sons of nobles went to the *calmecac,* a difficult school intended to prepare young men for leadership roles in religion and government.

Most young men were trained as warriors at a *telpochcalli.* Young women studied cloth making with a priestess at a temple. Both boys and girls also studied religion, dance, speech, crafts, and proper conduct. When the boys had proved themselves brave in battle, they left school and often went into the same work as their fathers. A girl usually left school when she married. She might become a market vendor, priestess, midwife, or healer.

When a young man was a good worker and a young woman was an able housekeeper, their parents arranged a marriage. Again there would be a celebration, with feasting, speeches, and predictions for the future. At the end of the ceremony, the young couple's clothing was knotted together to show they were joined.

Old age for the Aztecs was a time of rest and enjoyment. Old people were greatly respected for the contributions they had made, and their advice was valued.

Death was very important to the Aztecs because where the soul went after death was not determined by how one lived but by how one died. Bodies were usually burned, and then the soul went on a four-year jour-

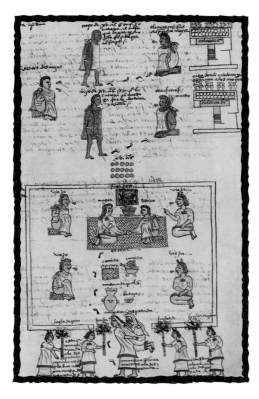

AN AZTEC PAINTING OF A
MARRIAGE CEREMONY. WITH
A PROCESSION OF FRIENDS,
THE MATCHMAKER CARRIES
THE BRIDE ON HER BACK TO
THE GROOM'S HOUSE. INSIDE,
THE PARENTS OF THE COUPLE
WATCH AS THE MATCHMAKER
MARRIES THE MAN AND
WOMAN BY TYING THE
CORNERS OF THEIR
CLOAKS TOGETHER.

ney with only a little dog as a guide. On this journey
the soul met many dangers—fierce jaguars, jagged
mountains, and wild rivers to cross. But finally the soul
would come to its special place in heaven.

If a woman died in childbirth or a man died bravely
in battle, their souls traveled with the sun. Some believed that if a warrior had been especially brave, he might
visit the earth as a hummingbird. People who drowned
lived with the rain god in the Paradise of Tlaloc. There
was a very special paradise in the heavens for children
and babies who died.

LIFE IN TENOCHTITLAN

Each day, as the sky above the mountains to the east of Tenochtitlan turned pink with the first light of morning, a figure climbed the steps to the top of the Great Pyramid. He lifted a conch shell to his lips and blasted the announcement that again the Aztec people had found favor with the gods. The sun had returned to journey across the sky.

The conch music flowed across Tenochtitlan and Lake Texcoco, and each household awakened. Everyone, from nobles to servants, rose from the straw mats they slept on to begin a new day.

Being neat and clean was important to the Aztecs. They often started the day with a steam bath. Afterward a man tied a loincloth around his waist and threw a

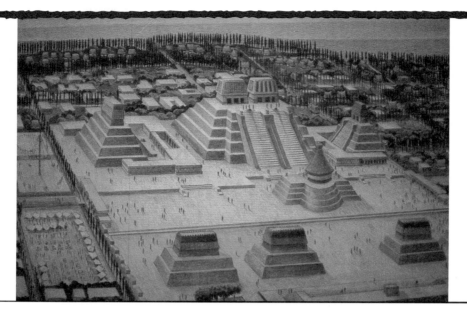

TENOCHTITLAN, THE AZTEC CAPITAL

cloak over one shoulder; a woman put on a long skirt and tunic. Sometimes women also wore triangle-shaped ponchos. Both men and women loved jewelry and wore earrings, necklaces, bracelets, and sometimes nose and lip plugs. Only the nobles wore sandals. The king's were made of gold. The higher a person was in Aztec society, the fancier and more beautifully embroidered his or her clothes were. Usually men wore their hair cut short in front and long in back. Women wore their hair in rolls on each side of the head.

Aztec breakfast usually meant corn porridge or corn cakes. Maize, or corn, was the staple food of the Aztecs.

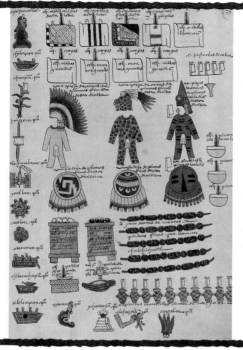

ITEMS SENT AS A TRIBUTE TO THE AZTECS FROM THE GULF COAST PROVINCE OF TOCHTEPEC. THIS WEALTHY PROVINCE GAVE DECORATED CLOTHING (TOP), WARRIORS' COSTUMES, GOLD ORNAMENTS (CENTER RIGHT), STRINGS OF JADE BEADS (CENTER), FEATHERS (LOWER LEFT), AND CHOCOLATE (LOWER RIGHT IN BASKETS). *FROM THE CODEX MENDOZA.*

They also grew squash, tomatoes, peppers, beans, jicama, prickly pear cactus, and sweet potatoes. They raised turkeys, ducks, and a type of small dog, but they ate meat only occasionally. They did eat foods found in the lake, such as fish, frogs, and insects. Bees were kept for honey. Chocolate was the favorite drink, but it was very expensive because cacao beans were also a form of money.

Among the Aztecs, one's work usually determined one's place in society. At the top were the nobles and priests who were leaders in religion, government, and war. Below them were the merchants who traveled throughout Mexico and Central America to supply Ten-

27.

TOP: PRIESTS SOUNDING A SNAKESKIN DRUM. THE WORK OF PRIESTS WAS HIGHLY VALUED IN AZTEC SOCIETY.

BOTTOM: AZTEC MERCHANTS FUNCTIONED AS REPORTERS OF WHAT WAS GOING ON IN OTHER PARTS OF MEXICO AND CENTRAL AMERICA AS THEY TRAVELED IN SEARCH OF WARES TO SELL IN TENOCHTITLAN.

ochtitlan with exotic goods. They also reported to the army all they saw and heard in the distant cities they visited.

Next came the artists, craftspeople, musicians, poets, and writers. The Aztecs were famous for their beautiful work in cloth making, embroidery, jewelry, and stone sculpture. Most famous were the beautiful designs made from tropical bird feathers and used in banners, head-dresses, cloaks, and decorations. The Aztecs kept very good records of their legends, history, and daily affairs in a *codex*, a type of book. These accordion-style books used a type of picture writing known as *hieroglyphics*.

MUSICIANS, AS WELL AS OTHER ARTISTS AND ARTISANS, PLAYED AN IMPORTANT ROLE IN AZTEC SOCIETY.

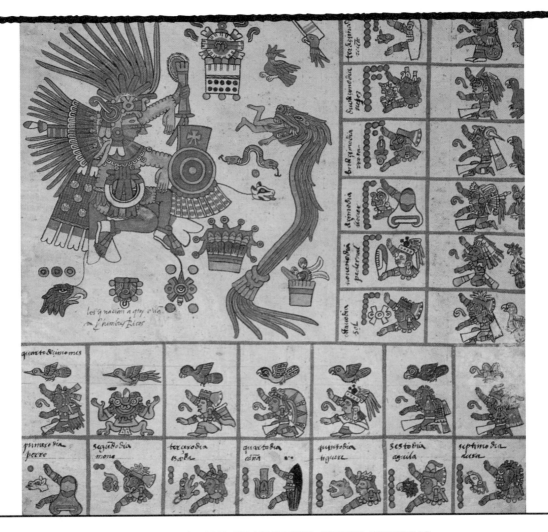

A FINE EXAMPLE OF ANOTHER CODEX, SHOWING
HIEROGLYPHICS. IN THE CENTER, THE GODS
TEZCALIPOCA AND QUETZALCOATL (GREEN
SERPENT) ARE DEVOURING A MAN.

Below the craftspeople were the common people: the shopkeepers, farmers, and fishermen. Slaves were considered to be the bottom of Aztec society. In Tenochtitlan, slaves were well-treated. They could earn money, own things, marry, and have families that were free. A slave could even own other slaves.

Most slaves were people who became slaves voluntarily. They usually needed to raise a large sum of money quickly, most often to pay off debts from betting on ball games. A person who committed a crime against another became that person's slave until the debt was paid. During the time of great famine, children were sold as slaves to a place where food was plentiful. The parents could get four or five hundred ears of corn for their family and be sure that their child had plenty to eat. When times were good again, they could buy the child back.

Being a slave was not a permanent thing. Slaves could be freed if their masters died, if they bought back their freedom, if they got others to substitute for them, if the term of service was over, or if they escaped from the slave market and ran to the king's palace without being caught.

The Aztecs loved the fun of competition, whether it was a slave's race for freedom, a practice battle, or a ball game. The Aztecs played many games, but hip ball was the favorite. Two teams tried to get a hard rubber

THE AZTECS LOVED GAMES OF ALL KINDS. HERE TWO PEOPLE ARE PLAYING A GAME CALLED PATOLLE.

63.

ball through a small hoop hung sideways on a wall. They used their hips, knees, and elbows to try to get the ball through the hoop.

The Aztecs developed a very accurate system to mark the passage of time. They had two calendars, one of 260 days for the religious year and one of 365 days for the solar year. The solar calendar was divided into eighteen months of twenty days each. Five unlucky days were added to the end of the year. The eighteen months were named for important events that happened in them, such as the time fruit falls. The days were named after important things in Aztec life: wind, rain, flower, reed, serpent.

A SCIENTIFIC RECONSTRUCTION OF THE AZTEC
CALENDAR, OR SUN STONE. THIS HUGE STONE
WEIGHED APPROXIMATELY TWENTY-FIVE
TONS AND WAS FOUND BURIED IN 1760.

Every fifty-two solar years, the first day of the two
calendars met. This was considered a very dangerous time.
The Aztecs believed that each of the past four suns ended
at the finish of one of these cycles. They also thought
that their present sun, the Sun of Movement, would be
destroyed at the end of a cycle in a flurry of earthquakes.

[43]

WHEN THE AZTECS' TWO CALENDARS (A RELIGIOUS ONE
AND A SOLAR ONE) COINCIDED EVERY FIFTY-TWO YEARS, THERE
WERE ELABORATE CEREMONIES TO THE GODS. WHEN
THE SUN ROSE THE FOLLOWING MORNING, PEOPLE
CELEBRATED AND REJOICED—THANKING THE GODS
FOR ALLOWING THEIR LIVES TO CONTINUE
FOR ANOTHER FIFTY-TWO YEARS.

At the end of fifty-two years, there were great ceremonies to the gods. At night all fires were put out. In total darkness the Aztecs waited, wondering, praying. Had they been strong enough? Honorable enough? Were their work and sacrifices over the past fifty-two years pleasing to the gods? Or would they die this night?

When the sun rose the next morning, the grateful Aztecs made a special sacrifice. A victim was taken to the top of the Great Pyramid, where the person's chest was slashed open with an *obsidian* knife. The heart was plucked out and burned, and a fire was started in the open chest. From this fire, new fires were lit throughout the city and countryside. People celebrated and thanked the gods for allowing their Sun to continue for at least another fifty-two years.

THE SPANISH COME

On April 21, 1519, Indians near Veracruz watched eleven giant white-winged towers sail to the gulf shore from the east. The men who came out of these towers had white skin and thick beards. Some were half men, half giant deer. With their magic, they could point a round tube of iron that made a loud noise, and whatever it pointed at would be destroyed. Trees burst apart. Holes were punched in mountains. Men died.

Messengers ran to tell the second King Moctezuma of these strange things. The Aztecs knew nothing of Europeans with sailing ships, guns, cannons, steel swords, and horses. Moctezuma and his advisors met and discussed what to do.

THE LANDING OF THE SPANIARDS. *FROM THE FLORENTINE CODEX, SIXTEENTH CENTURY, WRITTEN BY A MONK, BERNARDINO DE SAHAGÚN, ILLUSTRATED BY NATIVE ARTISTS.*

Moctezuma knew that this year was one of the times in the cycle of years that legend said Quetzalcoatl, the Plumed Serpent, might return to earth to rule his people. There had been many strange omens of his return during the past year. In the old codices, Quetzalcoatl had white skin and a beard and had sailed on a raft to the east. Could this be Quetzalcoatl coming back?

Seers and *soothsayers* began coming to Moctezuma. They had been having dreams, dreams of Tenochtitlan burning and falling apart stone by stone. Messengers brought more news of the strangers who were marching over the mountains to Tenochtitlan. The leader was called Hernán Cortés. Along the way he was knocking down temples of the brother and sister gods who had forced Quetzalcoatl to leave Mexico and replacing the temples with a cross. Surely, Moctezuma thought, these strangers were Quetzalcoatl or his representatives.

Moctezuma was almost crazy with worry and indecision. Some of his advisors said, "Attack. Do not let them in the city. We will be ruined." The two hundred thousand Aztec warriors could easily defeat the five hundred strangers. Others said, "Do not anger them. They must be gods and will destroy us if we displease them."

When the Spanish finally arrived at the crest of the hill above Tenochtitlan in November, they could hardly believe their eyes. In the valley below lay a huge city in the center of a lake. It was a city of beautiful monuments, gardens, and canals. It lay like a giant glistening jewel floating on the water. Never before had they seen such a beautiful and orderly city—not Paris, not London, not Madrid, not Rome. They were all villages compared to Tenochtitlan. More than a million people lived in the island city and on the shores of Lake Texcoco.

Moctezuma decided to greet Hernán Cortés and the Spaniards as friends and welcome them to Tenochtitlan with a celebration. The Spanish stayed in the palace reserved for important guests. They were given great feasts and beautiful gifts of gold, precious stones, embroidery, and featherworks. They were shown all of the city and allowed to visit the temples.

Soon Moctezuma realized that Cortés was not a representative of Quetzalcoatl, but he did not know what these strange people wanted. Moctezuma hoped that if he gave the Spaniards enough presents they could be bribed to go away. He gave them more of the gold they seemed to like so much, including a helmet filled with gold dust and a gold carving of the sun several feet in diameter. But the golden gifts only made the Spaniards want more. Moctezuma didn't know that the Spaniards felt they were on God's mission to save Indian souls and believed that any gold or wealth they might find was God's way of repaying them for their good deeds.

After one week in Tenochtitlan, Hernán Cortés took Moctezuma and his family prisoners and made Moctezuma announce to all of the people that Cortés was now in charge. The city and all of its treasures now belonged to the Spanish. Cortés melted down beautifully carved gold jewelry and religious symbols and sent the gold and other Aztec treasures back to Spain.

Months later, during an Aztec holy day celebration when Cortés was temporarily gone from Tenochtitlan, Spanish soldiers began to fear that the dancing Aztecs

[49]

CORTÉS MEETING MOCTEZUMA. THE ARRIVAL OF THE
SPANIARDS WAS THE BEGINNING OF THE
END OF THE AZTEC CIVILIZATION.

were getting ready to attack. They massacred hundreds of unarmed dancers. Chaos followed. Somehow Moctezuma was killed—stoned by his own people, the Spanish said; murdered by the Spanish, said the Aztecs. Both Aztecs and Spanish, who had come to respect Moctezuma, mourned his death.

This time it was the Aztecs' turn to attack. Warriors dressed in their animal costumes of heavily quilted cotton soaked in brine to make it stiff and strong. They put on their wild headdresses and face paint. They picked up shields, bows and arrows, knives, spears, and the deadly flat clubs that had blades of obsidian, volcanic glass, embedded along the edges. These clubs were so sharp that an Aztec could behead a horse in one swipe.

The Spanish fled, but first the soldiers filled their pockets and cloaks with Aztec gold and treasures. The Aztecs destroyed the causeway and canal bridges. The soldiers were forced to jump and swim. The weight of the stolen gold drowned soldier after soldier, until so many bodies filled the canals that the remaining soldiers could scramble across them to shore. This battle became known as the Night of Sorrows.

Cortés planned a new attack. He enlisted the aid of the Indian tribes that the Aztecs had conquered and heavily taxed. They surrounded Tenochtitlan and cut off all supplies. Starvation and smallpox swept through the city.

THE SPANIARDS PLUNDERED AND DESTROYED UNTIL
NOTHING WAS LEFT OF THE BEAUTIFUL
CITY OF TENOCHTITLAN.

For eighty days this *siege* continued. In a final attack the Spanish and the Indians assisting them fought with the Aztecs until the canal waters of Tenochtitlan ran red with blood. Two hundred forty thousand Aztecs died during the siege.

After the final surrender, the Spanish soldiers knocked down all of the temples and the serpent wall looking for gold and jewels that were rumored to be buried in their foundations. They gathered all of the treasure they could find and some Aztec curiosities, including the now treasured codices, and sent them to Spain. Everything else they burned. Not a building was left standing. The beautiful city of Tenochtitlan was truly dead.

THE AZTECS' LEGACY

The day after the Aztecs' surrender there was a violent thunderstorm. Aztec legends say it was caused by the gods fleeing Tenochtitlan forever. In their place came the Spanish missionaries. To stamp out any traces of the Aztec religion, they built their churches on top of Aztec temple ruins, often using rubble from the temples.

Many of the Spanish soldiers chose to stay in Mexico and marry Indian women, starting a new race of Mexican people who are of both Spanish and Indian descent. They took large tracts of land for their ranches and forced their Indian allies to work for them like *serfs*. Most Indians found they were worse off under Spanish rule than they had been under the Aztecs.

Although today there are many statues and monuments in Mexico honoring Moctezuma and other Aztec leaders, there are none of Cortés. Many feel he destroyed one of the most advanced civilizations and one of the most beautiful cities of the world. The Mexican people are very proud of their Indian heritage and of the great things the Aztecs were able to create from so little. Even today many Mexican and American customs, crafts, and foods come from the Aztecs. Among the foods that have come to us are tortillas, tamales, chocolate, domestic turkey, tomatoes, and avocados. Some Aztec customs and crafts still with us are cloth weaving and elaborately styled embroidery and the well-ordered market layout.

The Aztecs are often looked upon as barbaric because of their practice of human sacrifice. But in all of their history as a nation they did not kill as many people as the Spanish did during the struggle for Tenochtitlan, when they were saving souls and gathering gold.

The Aztecs believed that life comes from death. The sacrificed heart bled so that the sun could travel across the sky to provide for the living. Today Mexico City stands on the exact spot where Tenochtitlan stood. The Zocalo, the city center of Mexico City, is on paved-over ruins of the sacred square in the center of Tenochtitlan. The Great Cathedral and the President's Palace, built by the Spanish, stand where the Great Pyramid and Montezuma's palace once stood. Lake Texcoco has been

THE RUINS OF AZTEC TEMPLES IN ZOCALO, THE CITY
CENTER OF MEXICO CITY. THIS AREA WAS THE
SACRED SQUARE IN THE CENTER OF TENOCHTITLAN.

THIS TEMPLE ATOP A PYRAMID IS THE
ONLY ONE TO SURVIVE THE SPANISH
CONQUEST—A SAD LEGACY.

drained, but major streets run the routes of the old causeways and canals.

In 1978 the foundation of the Great Pyramid was discovered at the corner of the Zocalo, between the Great Cathedral and the President's Palace. It is being *excavated,* and in 1988 it was opened to the public so that we may walk through the ruins, stand where the sacrificial victims stood, look up at the steep steps that once rose into the heavens, and know that out of death comes life. Out of the death of Tenochtitlan has sprung the beautiful and vibrant Mexico City, one of the largest cities in the world.

Above the Zocalo flies the Mexican flag. The country was named for the Aztecs, for it is only in recent years that the group of people that Hummingbird Wizard renamed the Mexicas have once again become known as the Aztecs. In the center of that flag is a picture of a prickly pear cactus with red fruit, growing out of a rock. Perched on top of the cactus is an eagle eating a serpent. As Hummingbird Wizard promised, this marks the place where a great civilization would be built.

GLOSSARY

Aqueduct   a large pipe or canal carrying water

Barbarian   not civilized; rough and bad-mannered

Calmecac (kal-ME-kak)   an advanced school where specially talented boys learned to be priests and leaders

Causeway   a raised roadway built over marshy or wet lowlands

Chinampas (chee-NAM-paz)   large floating rafts of dirt used for farming

Codex (plural: codices)   an accordion-style Aztec book of picture writing

Excavate   to unearth or carefully dig up historical ruins

Hieroglyphics a style of writing using pictures and symbols instead of words

Obsidian a dark, glassy volcanic rock that can be cut to be very sharp

Prophesy to predict a future event

Sacrifice an offering to the gods

Seers and soothsayers people who see or foretell the future, often using signs such as dreams or comets and other things in nature

Serf someone who works in the fields for a master

Siege to surround a city or fort during war and cut off all trading, including food and water supplies

Telpochcalli (tel-poch-KA-lee) regular school for all Aztec teenagers

Teomamaque specially chosen priests who carry images of gods or the containers said to be the home of the gods' spirits

FOR FURTHER READING

Berdan, Frances F. *The Aztecs*. New York: Chelsea House, 1989.

de Gerez, Toni. *My Song Is a Piece of Jade: Poems of Ancient Mexico in English and Spanish*. Boston: Little, Brown and Co., 1984.

Glubok, Shirley, ed. *The Fall of the Aztecs*. New York: St. Martin's, 1965.

Karen, Ruth. *Feathered Serpent: The Rise and Fall of the Aztecs*. New York: Four Winds, 1979.

Leon-Potilla, Miguel, ed. *The Broken Spears: The Aztec Account of the Conquest of Mexico*. Boston: Beacon Press, 1962.

Marrin, Albert. *Aztecs and Spaniards: Cortes and the Conquest of Mexico*. New York: Atheneum, 1986.

Steel, Anne. *An Aztec Warrior*. Vero Beach, Fl: Rourke Enterprises, Inc., 1988.

Stuart, Gene S. *The Mighty Aztecs*. Washington, D.C.: The National Geographic Society, 1981.

INDEX

ABOUT THE AUTHOR

Donna Walsh Shepherd lives and writes in Anchorage, Alaska, and teaches at the University of Alaska. She first became fascinated with the Aztecs as an elementary school student and has traveled in Mexico studying their history and culture.